EXTREME MAKEOVER
HOW TO STAY
Spiritually
FIT

NEW BIRTH PUBLISHING

EMPOWER • ENCOURAGE • EDUCATE

Published by New Birth Publishing
ISBN-13:978-0692692790
ISBN-10:0692692797

Extreme Makeover
How to Stay

Spiritually
FIT

C. D. McMillan

Contents

Dedication

**To my Pastor, Friend,
and Grandmother:**
Dr. Ruby L. Eldridge,
Pastor/Founder of Pure Word Ministries, Inc.
You are my inspiration.

To my Mom & Dad,
Valerie & Rev. Cedrick McMillan

Keep holding on to God's unchanging hand.
I love you both, and welcome back into my life.

To

Judy Napp:

Continue transforming lives that you touch.
Your input into my life many years ago
has caused a great difference
in what could have been my outcome.

Acknowledgements

Mostly, I thank God for
directing me in the writing of this book.
For without Him I could do NOTHING!

To all my family and friends who
supported me in this endeavor
to encourage the Body of Christ.

To Jannie Hampton, and
Pastor O'Neil Porter
for aiding in preparing this book.

To Rev. Dr. Classy Preston, pastor of Pleasant
Grove Church, Cary, NC, for sharing
the vision of this book and writing the
Foreword.

Foreword

I am honored to introduce the work of my nephew, C.D. McMillan, a young man who has been intentional about seeking God. As I read his story, I could see the handiwork of God in motion and the many ways God answers his prayers. I identified with many of his struggles because we really grew up in the same environment with similar challenges. This work is a great effort to help others assess their relationship with God while in and beyond the church. Each individual chapter provides an opportunity to hear the voice of a young man who has openly confronted his demons by calling them out by name. His honesty and openness are refreshment to the soul.

We live in a society filled with temptations which lure us away from God, and often we are failures in spiritual warfare. Unfortunately, we are not spiritually equipped to fight back. Therefore, we live unproductive lives and limit our intimacy with God.

Pastor McMillan provides specific instructions and weapons to be used for our success. As you move through the chapters, you will be equipped to empower others in your immediate and church families. This young, wise man has given us a personal view from the pew, and this resource is a gift from God for us all.

Dr. Classy Preston
Senior Pastor • Pleasant Grove Church
Cary, NC 27519

Preface

After much prayer and fasting, I felt lead to write this book to encourage the Body of Christ. Being a minister, and having the opportunity to see my maternal grandmother pastor a church, I have the privilege to encounter believers all over the United States. Being in Church has taught me that even though I preach on Sunday morning, I can be barely hanging on to God by Monday morning. I wrote this book to encourage the Body of Christ to learn to shed the unnecessary weight that is keeping us from the blessings of God. Even in my walk with God, I have had to re-examine where I was. This fast-paced society has taught us that we need things fast. Yet, after the instant gratification we are left empty. While getting ready to write this book, I ran across a quote by Eugene Peterson. Peterson's quote fell in line with what I was seeing the church as today. Peterson said, "Many claim to have been born again, but the evidence for mature Christian discipleship is slim. There is a great market for religious experience in our world; there is little enthusiasm for the patient acquisition of virtue, little inclination to sign up for a long apprenticeship in what earlier generations of Christians called holiness."

As a spiritual leader, I see the importance of being spiritually fit. God has sent His Son to die for us, so that we can have eternal life. Therefore, it is necessary for us to have a close relationship with Christ. We can not just know about Him, we must have a relationship with Him. If we plan to reign with Him we must do what we have to do to get ready to meet Him. We are His bride and we must prepare for our wedding day with Him! It is my sincere prayer that this book will give you insight on how to properly engage in a spiritual workout that will lead you to every blessing that God has promised you.

~C. D. McMillan

Introduction

As long as I can remember, I have always wanted to be a part of the church. I can still remember being seven years old and wearing a robe, not a suit, to church. I was fascinated with the singing, shouting, and preaching. I can still remember being the "preacher," when I played church with other kids in my neighborhood. Church was a big part of my life. I was reared by my maternal grandmother. Her rule for attending church was mandatory. It was in church that I learned valuable lessons. The most valuable lesson learned is the necessity of being real. As I have matured in my faith, I see the church differently than I did when I was seven years old. I understand that there is so much more to God than shouting, singing, and preaching. When I was seven years old, I was more into emotions and the outward aspects of the church. I wore a robe to church every Sunday because I wanted so badly to be able to make the people shout and say, "Amen," like the pastor. I saw the robe as a sign of power. I was in awe of how the preacher could get the people excited and give money, even when they knew they had bills due. However, today I see that under the robe there must be a life of Christ being lived. The robe does not and will not make a preacher. One must be called, and anointed. If you are called and anointed then God will make provision for the vision.

My earliest memories of the church were that of judging the outer core of people. That was a big mistake. The Bible says, *"Man looks at the outer appearances, but GOD looks at the heart!"* Being brought up in a strict Pentecostal Church, I was more judgmental than a judge and more an "aint" than a "saint." I was not taught to see what God focuses on, the heart of mankind. Many share this same experience. By the time I entered my preaching ministry, I labeled every woman in pants and cosmetics a "Jezebel," and thought a "good time" at church was determined by emotionalism (people falling out & shouting) and/or we had a long drawn out service. I am not sure where the Jezebel labeling came from, but I do know it was heavily preached in the strict Pentecostal church. Now that I have learned the word for myself, I now know that it was a lack of proper studying of scripture. If read carefully, we see that a true Jezebel spirit is a spirit of control. Jezebel was not destroyed by God because she had "painted eyes." Rather, she was destroyed because she brought idol gods into Israel and killed God's prophets. It seems ludicrous today that I had that mindset about being a Child of God. I can truly relate to the old congregational song, "Look where He's brought me from...He's brought me out of darkness into His marvelous light!" That song is a testimony. Those words speak to all of us. God will, if we allow him too, bring us all out of our darkness. For God is the Light. The lack of knowledge comes from the lack of time with God. No relationship equals no revelation. I can remember when I had begun preaching, I thought that because God had called me that I had "made it" spiritually. I was sadly mistaken. I went through a dry spot for a while. Leading up to my initial sermon, I fasted, prayed, and meditated on the Word. In a sense I became relaxed. I got the mentality that "I had made it." For a long time, I questioned God about whether or not I was in the right calling. I was in the right calling, but I just was not doing what it took to make it successful. Now that I pray, fast, and read the Word consistently, my ministry has blossomed. I am able to hear God's voice clearly and can feel the anointing, not an emotion, every time I enter into His Temple. I have found it to be factual that God is pure love. Jesus Christ is the blue print for our Christian life. Sadly, instead of building our Christian life by God's blueprints, we have tried to cut corners. In doing so, we have not built a beautiful masterpiece. We have only built an abstract, and that is not what God designed! We all have got to train ourselves to "go back" to the blueprints God has given us and start building correctly. A structure that is not built correctly will not survive a storm. We have to make sure our relationship with God is solid. If it is not, it is time for us to refer to the blueprints and see where we have gone wrong.

A structure that is not built correctly will not survive a storm.

I believe the Church today has failed most believers in that we seek for something deeper when Salvation is mere acceptance of Christ. Our relationship with God is not confined to a certain way or form. It is a commitment that comes with a sacrifice. I think Kirk Franklin said it best in his song, "Let It Go." The song states that "church taught me how to shout and how to speak in tongues, but preacher, teach me how to live now when the tongue is done." Being saved is easy, it is staying saved that is a challenge. Today, there are so many outside distractions. We desire to stay spiritually fit, but all around us are harmful spirits trying to lure us into a lifestyle of spiritual laxity. The struggle is transforming our minds and appetites to the Word of God. We go through withdrawals like sugar and carb addicts. Our flesh craves for the lust of this world, which our Great Physician has given us a guideline to maintaining a healthy and abundant life. It is a constant tug-of-war. We have the desire to have the same faith and power as the old saints, but we have gotten too consumed in the "modern" church that we find it so hard to return to the old way. Today, we have found a way to justify everything. To old saints, any untruth is a lie. Today, we say, "I did not want to hurt his/her feelings." The views of the old saints were directly aligned with the Word of God. It may not have made sense to us, then and now, but they were able to get through to God. We have tried to live a double life for so long that when we cannot pleasure our flesh we find a way to do what we want anyway. What is so interesting to me is that today, we can see when people are going through in the church. They come to church with a lemon face and outwardly show that they are hurting. Instead of worshiping God and believing that God is in control, they will seek man for a solution. My grandmother always reminds us that when old saints came to church they came only to praise God, not to broadcast their problems. They understood that they were one day closer to their deliverance. They understood the power of prayer, fasting, and praise. If we have the will to be spiritually healthy, we will avoid the "goodies" of this world. This lifestyle is personal. It is not about trying to impress others, only God. This lifestyle change obligates us to take up the cross everyday. We are to do exactly what Paul instructs us to do, which is to lay aside every {hindrance} that keeps us from following after Christ. (Hebrews 12:1) We must be consistent to achieve the prize (the Crown of Glory). Our need to be spiritually fit determines our eternity. As long as we eat the right foods and drink water, our skin, hair, and bodies are in great shape. This also serves our spiritual life. When we sacrifice the junk foods of life (gossip, lust, sexual immorality, etc.) we will be able to grow and be in good health. We must remember that we will all stand before the judgment seat of Christ. It is time for us to take our spiritual health seriously. We are both spirit and flesh. Therefore, we must take care of both. We focus so much on trying to look good physically that our spiritual man is abandoned. That is why 1 Timothy 4:8 tells us, *"For bodily exercise profiteth little: but godliness is profitable unto all things, having promise of the life that now is, and of that which is to come."*

You see we must be spiritually fit for eternal life. Physical obesity leads to death, but spiritual obesity leads to eternal damnation. We must be ready for the bridegroom. Any woman who is getting married will tell you that they want to look their best on their wedding day. Therefore, we need to do all we can to walk Godly. It is walking Godly that is "profitable for all things!"

Many of us are killing our spirit man and do not even realize it until we are in a critical state. For instance 5lb – 7lbs can easily slip on us and our response is almost always, "I did not know I gained so much weight." We have failed to eat properly. Hebrews 5:13-14 (NIV) says,

> *13 Anyone who lives on milk, being still an infant, is not acquainted with the teaching about righteousness.*
>
> *14 But solid food is for the mature, who by constant use have trained themselves to distinguish good from evil.*

In order to be fit for the Kingdom we have got to eat properly. Moreover, Jesus reminds us in Matthew 5:8: "This people draweth nigh unto me with their mouth, and honoureth me with their lips; but their heart is far from me."

Today, obesity has become one of the leading health concerns in American society. Obesity can lead to some of the following health complications:

- Diabetes

- heart disease and/or stroke

- gallbladder disease

- osteoarthritis (degeneration of cartilage and bone of joints)

- sleep apnea and other breathing problems

- some forms of cancer (uterine, breast, colorectal, kidney, and gallbladder)

Moreover, statistics from the Wellness International Network show:

- 58 Million Overweight; 40 Million Obese; 3 Million morbidly Obese

- Eight out of 10 over 25's Overweight

- 78% of American's not meeting basic activity level recommendations

- 25% completely Sedentary

- 76% increase in Type II diabetes in adults 30-40 yrs old since 1990.

Not only is obesity a health problem, it is also a financial problem. Each year millions of dollars are wasted because of obesity. Sadly, the "church" has many of the same statistics. We are so spiritually overweight that it is difficult to fast, pray, and enjoy our walk with Christ as we did before.

According to the American Diabetes Association, "Diabetes is a disease in which the body does not produce or properly use insulin. Insulin is a hormone that is needed to convert sugar, starches and other food into energy needed for daily life." Spiritually, diabetes represents our inactive prayer life. Without Prayer, we are unable to go through the struggles of this life. Our spirit man is not able to have a direct line with God, thus hindering our ability to have a deep personal relationship with God. The strongest Christian is one who stays on his/her knees. When we have a strong prayer life, we are able to bombard Heaven and get results.

When we have a strong prayer life, we are able to bombard Heaven and get results.

Heart disease and stroke are also ravaging health concerns in our society. One of the things about heart problems is that they often go undetected until it's too late. People with heart conditions can look strong and fit on the outside, but are one heart beat closer to death. I have known people to be in shape physically, but deep down in their heart, arteries and veins were clogged. That blockage went undetected, and one day without warning, they died. The same principle of heart disease applies to us spiritually. We, as Christians, believe we are spiritually fit, but our hearts do not really belong to God. We have to remember that scripture tell us, "If any man among you seem to be religious, and bridleth not his tongue, but deceiveth his own heart, this man's religion is vain."(James 1:26) In not giving Christ our heart completely, we only deceive ourselves, thus our religion is in vain. Without giving Christ our hearts completely, we will not be able to walk in a right relationship with Him. Without that relationship, Christ does not know our voice. In order for God to bless us, He must know who we are. Without that relationship, He doesn't. Deuteronomy 6:5 declares, *"Love the LORD your God with all your heart and with all your soul and with all your strength."* And when Jesus taught the people what God expected, Jesus said, *"Love the Lord your God with all your heart and with all your soul and with all your mind. This is the first and greatest commandment." And the second is like it, which is to love your neighbor as yourself.* (Matthew 22:37-40)

We need to examine who has our heart today. If it is not God, it is time to give it to Him completely. Only a skilled doctor can repair the blockage in the heart, and that doctor is the Great Physician, JESUS! The Prophet Isaiah recounted the Lord's words, which were: These people come near to me with their mouth and honor me with their lips, but their hearts are far from me. Their worship of me is made up only of rules taught by men. (Isaiah 29:13) I encourage you to make sure God has your heart, because if He does not, a spiritual heart attack or stroke will come up unexpectedly.

We experience spiritual cancer when we allow ungodly things to set up in our minds, hearts, and souls. Cancer cells are cells that are abnormal. Anything that is not of God is abnormal. If we have any cancer cells, we need to begin radiation. We need to seek God and allow Him to remove all imperfections in us. He told us that we will go into the fire and come out as pure gold.

We have "played" church long enough. We have enjoyed the junk food (our hindrances), but it is time to start eating properly. It is time to eat some real substance that will make our spirituality stronger. We are told we are not to "live by bread alone but by every word that comes from the mouth of the LORD". (Deut. 8:3) If we eat properly, we are able to reap the promises God has for us. God has told us to be one thing, and that one thing is HOLY. This applies to all Christians. No matter your denomination, we are called to be HOLY. First Peter 1:16 says, *"Be ye holy; for I am holy."* Even if you read it backwards, the Word remains the same: Holy am I; Holy ye be! Holiness is not a denomination; it is a way of life. We are to be Holy in all aspects of our life. It is not a Sunday experience, but it is a daily walk with God.

> *We experience spiritual cancer when we allow ungodly things to set up in our minds, hearts, and souls.*

We are so consumed in this "must-have," "must-see" society. We need to learn to be good stewards of our time and energy. For too long we have focused on the wrong things. Paul instructs in the letter to the Galatian church that we reap what we sow. Reaping is planting in expectation to receive something in return. It does not happen over night; it is a process. All the mischievous things we have sown will come back to us. You do not become overweight overnight. Obesity happens from years of abusive behavior to our bodies, which leads to complications and addictions. The same applies to our spirit man. We have allowed so much to be consumed that it is detrimental to our health. We pray and fast only for material things. There is no longer all night prayer and weekly fasts to strip our flesh and strengthen our spirit man. We often quote Romans 8:39 concerning what shall separate us from the love of God, but the truth is we have some things in our lives that we know exists that separate us from God's guidance and wisdom. Thus, we allow things to separate us from God. We say we want His love, but we withhold our love and commitment from Him. We think God owes us, but the reality is He does not need us; we need Him. We need to remember that. We have forgotten the words of the Prophet Jeremiah. In Jeremiah 8:21-23, Jeremiah is trying to get the people to realize the cures they have available to them. Gilead had the "balm." They were just too caught up to realize it. Just as the Children of Israel were stubborn, we are too. We do not realize we have Christ today as our healing balm.

The Old Hymn says:
There is a balm in Gilead
to make the wounded whole.
There is a balm in Gilead
to heal the sin-sick soul.

This hymn acknowledges that we need help. We cannot walk this Christian life alone.

Now we say we are "soldiers in the army of the Lord," but our actions do not speak as a soldier. A soldier has commitment. A soldier's will becomes the will of whom he/she serves. A soldier takes every obstacle that comes his/her way. They are driven! They are focused! Each day they drink plenty of water and eat properly! They train their bodies to be machines. Why? They endure the training, because they know and understand the goal. Therefore, they welcome the rigorous workouts and training. When the drill sergeant orders more training time, they do it. It is hard work, but they do it because it is for their own good (when they are on the battlefield) and it will bring them closer to their goal (defending their country from enemies). We compare ourselves to soldiers. Why can't we, and why won't we, take up their work ethic? We need to learn how to check ourselves and see how much training and exercise we really need. Many of us have not been productive in the ministry since we "found Jesus." We are in the same spot we were in when God saved us. When Moses died, God gave the children of Israel

> *The Christian life is not a playground; it is a battlefield.*

11

thirty days to mourn. When it was up, God instructed them to MOVE! Sitting does not help us unless we are in the presence of God. Living is being active. God cannot use us sitting down! It is time for us to get up from the pew and start working out. The Christian life is not a playground; it is a battlefield. The worst part for us, as Christians, is that our enemy cannot be seen. Remember, *"For we wrestle not against flesh and blood, but against principalities, against powers, against the rulers of the darkness of this world, against spiritual wickedness in high places"*. (Ephesians 6:12)

In the medical world, doctors use a caliper to measure how much body fat a person has. The caliper pinches the skin and registers a number. This then is compared to their height. The result of the comparison determines if a person is overweight. We need to pinch ourselves with the Word of God. The Word will pinch and pierce you, if you are in error. I guarantee many, if not all of us, will find ourselves obese. The truth is, we are going to miss out on the Kingdom of Heaven if we don't get this sinful foolishness out of us. We are overweight because we have allowed spirits to dominate our minds and bodies. Remember John 8:32 tells us, *"And ye shall know the truth, and the truth shall make you free."*

Check the list and see how we measure up:
- The gossiping spirit
- The lying spirit
- The unforgiving spirit
- The homosexual/lesbian spirit
- The cheating spirit

- The robbing spirit
- The fornicating spirit
- The "playing church" spirit
- The deceitful spirit
- The jealously spirit
- The poverty spirit
- The division spirit
- The manipulation spirit
- The judgmental spirit
- The "I need more" spirit
- The depression spirit
- The settling for less spirit
- The backbiting spirit
- The coveting spirit
- The complaining spirit
- The arrogant spirit
- The "I don't believe in tithing" spirit
- The "I know it all" spirit

Those are just a few of the spirits that we have not purged from our bodies. Because we have not gotten rid of them, they have caused us to be, and stay overweight.

You might not be overweight with any of the spirits listed above, but I promise you if you search deep you will find some other ones. We, alone, have allowed ourselves to be obese.

Recently, our church purchased a new church van. As I was test driving it, I noticed some writing on the passenger side-window. It read: objects in mirror are closer than they appear. I have never paid much attention to those words before. At that moment I began to see those words in a spiritual sense. We do not believe that things are close to us, but the reality is they are. That is why the Bible instructs us to "pray without ceasing." (1 Thess. 5:17) We go on for so long not paying attention to how often we do not fast, pray, and spend time with God. Before long we can not make a solid connection with God. Like Samson, we have lost our power. That is why we must always be watchful. We have got to monitor ourselves and make sure we are on the right track, because if we do not we will not be able to see the enemy coming to attack us. Just like in the side window of our cars, if we do not pay attention, we will hit something. Spiritually we have to be on guard so that the enemy will not cause us to crash and loose what we have worked so hard to get.

I believe we all have the ability to make our walk with God a lifestyle. Spirituality is not a one time altar experience. It is a daily walk with God. Paul admits, "I must die daily." (1 Cor. 15:31) If we do not, we will be totally consumed by demonic spirits. We too must do the same thing. I can remember my aunt trying the Atkins Diet a few years ago to shed some pounds. She lost the weight, but after a few months, she gained her old weight plus additional weight. This happened because she did not make a lifestyle change. She did it for awhile but eventually went back to her old ways of eating. Spiritually, we have done the same thing. The Bible says, "No man can serve two masters: for either he will hate the one, and love the other;

or else he will hold to the one, and despise the other. Ye cannot serve God and mammon." (Matthew 6:24) We must truly love this Christian lifestyle and hate the lifestyle of our flesh which leads to damnation. We cannot start this lifestyle change until we rid ourselves of old habits and urges. The problem is that we do not see obstacles as a help to us; we only see them as hindrances. We give up easily and get discouraged. We tell ourselves that we have done our best to make ourselves feel better, but the reality is we really have not tried at all. We tell ourselves we cannot before we even try. We say, "I cannot pray; I cannot fast; I cannot sow a seed, etc." We stop the possibility of success before we even try. It has bothered me that as "saints," we find it so hard to hold onto our focus, to keep our goal in sight, and to keep working like a soldier. We have to welcome challenges as a soldier in order to achieve victory. If we would accept life's challenges as a gift sent by God to make us stronger, we would be able to start the process of purging ourselves from the junk food. For, a spiritual workout would lead us to a brighter future on Earth, and most importantly in Heaven. Remember, we are not here to stay. Eternity is forever. We have an option today to choose our final destination: heaven or hell. When Jesus is our focus, our battles become small.

The devil has deceived many of us. He has been successful in attacking our mind. We are so sure we are saved, sanctified, Holy-Ghost filled, fire baptized with Jesus on our mind and on our way to heaven. That is a lie. When Jesus comes back there are going to be two types of people in the world, aints and saints. Going to heaven is going to cost us sacrifice. It is going to be the people that really have a love for God that are going to make it to heaven. The sad thing is that God wants us all to take part in heaven, but WE are hindering his plan for us. 1 John 1:1-10 says:

1   *That which was from the beginning, which we have heard, which we have seen with our eyes, which we have looked upon, and our hands have handled, of the Word of life;*

2   *For the life was manifested, and we have seen it, and bear witness, and shew unto you that eternal life, which was with the Father, and was manifested unto us;*

3   *That which we have seen and heard declare we unto you, that ye also may have fellowship with us: and truly our fellowship is with the Father, and with his Son Jesus Christ.*

4   *And these things write we unto you, that your joy may be full.*

5   *This then is the message which we have heard of him, and declare unto you, that God is light, and in him is no darkness at all.*

6   *If we say that we have fellowship with him, and walk in darkness, we lie, and do not the truth:*

7   *But if we walk in the light, as he is in the light, we have fellowship one with another, and the blood of Jesus Christ his Son cleanseth us from all sin.*

8   *If we say that we have no sin, we deceive ourselves, and the truth is not in us.*

9   *If we confess our sins, he is faithful and just to forgive us our sins, and to cleanse us from all unrighteousness.*

10 *If we say that we have not sinned, we make him a liar, and his word is not in us.*

The writer of 1 John warned the saints of the early church of examining themselves. Then and now the Word still applies. Many of us only have a form of godliness. (2 Timothy 3:5) We have not confessed our sins (1 John 1:6); we have not responded to the Word (1 John 2:4); we have no love for others (1 John 2:11); and we have not practiced righteousness (1 John 3:8). It is so easy to think we are something, but really are not anything at all.

I am reminded of a story about a young soldier that fought for Alexander the Great. One day this soldier was brought before Alexander the Great because he ran away from a battle. Because of his age, Alexander the Great was beginning to take pity on him until he found out the soldiers name. When the soldier told Alexander the Great that his name was also Alexander, Alexander the Great picked him up and threw him down and told him to change his conduct or change his name!

That story applies to us. We need to change the way we live or stop calling ourselves a Christian. We need to admit to ourselves that we are spiritually unfit and full of many demonic spirits. As the writer of 1 John points out, we only deceive ourselves when we feel that we are no sinner. The problem today is that we have sinned and done what we want for so long that we have come to believe we are right. Many of us, yes Saints of God, have done wrong for so long that we no longer feel convicted about things. We are no longer humble as the saints of old. Those saints LIVED a life. They may not have had the money, cars, or clothes, but they had a connection with God.

There was a little country church seeking a new pastor and they had narrowed their choice down to two preachers. One preacher was an older man who had no theological degrees and the other was a younger educated preacher. When it came down to choosing the new pastor, the church unanimously chose the older uneducated preacher. The young educated preacher was shocked because he just knew he would be selected. The chairman of the deacon board told the young preacher, "We chose the older preacher because he knows the Lord and not just about Him." Education, money, and talent do not give us a relationship with Christ. In order to reign with God there must be a relationship established. Many people know me, but do not have a relationship with me. Many of us know facts about Christ, but have no personal relationship with Him. We have to live a life so that others will know whom we serve.

Gordon D. Venturella said, "False spirituality—spirituality that sits back, procrastinates, is lazy and then blames God or other people for the mess that they get in. This kind of spirituality is more magical thinking than true spirituality. This kind of magical thinking is bathed in artificial christianeese language, views the Bible as a magical charm, and God as a genie in a bottle waiting for us to come up with the right magical incantations so He'll do our bidding."

We are to all have a testimony. We sing, "*I am a living testimony,*" but we are not living it. A testimony is an experience a witness tells about. When we received Christ we were to tell others. When the Samaritan woman had an experience with Christ, she ran and told others about Jesus. To live for Jesus requires us to bear fruit. We cannot and will not bear fruit if we are obese. In order to actively walk with Christ we have got to be living out the characteristics of Christ. Therefore we should be living the life of Love, Hope, and Faith. The writer of 1 John has warned us to search ourselves. If we do not get it together, in hell will we lift up our eyes.

Many of us have delayed our blessings because we have been immobile to receive them. Obesity limits mobility; there fore, the weight must come off. We, alone, have crippled ourselves.

God's Word will reverse the damage we have caused. We did it to ourselves, therefore we have two choices: 1) Engage in Spiritual workout (extreme makeover) that can save us from eternal damnation or 2) Continue to live each day obese, which will only send us to one place, hell. I am sure you chose option one. The road will not be easy, but He did promise NEVER to leave us. Therefore, we must take on the soldier's mentality of defeating the enemy.

We cannot and will not bear fruit if we are obese.

Paul says, "I CAN DO ALL THINGS THROUGH CHRIST WHICH STRENGTHENS ME!" (Phil. 4:13)   Bob the Builder has a saying: "Can We Do It?" The answer is, "YES! We Can!" Why? Because if God be for us, what can be against us? I do not know about you, but I am ready to walk into my season and into the blessings God has laid up for me. So, soldier, get ready. The workout is about to begin. God is the Drill

Sergeant and he has given us our workout manual to follow, which is the Bible. Study it, and take heed and I promise you the weight will fall off. Most importantly, if you become a "doer and not just a hearer" of His instructions, you will be able to keep the weight off.   If you do that, you will be able to undergo a fulfilled and healthy lifestyle change. So get ready for an Extreme Makeover! It is a sure way to abundant living.

Chapter One:
The Warm Up Exercise
Stretching

As with any workout, you must begin with stretching. Stretching is important because it reduces the chances of developing cramps during a workout. For our spiritual workout, our stretching is undergoing the process of forgiveness. This is a three-fold process. In the process, our first task is true repentance. Christ has never changed, but we have. He has always been there waiting for us to come in for our checkup. Repentance is a process in which we are declaring to God that we have sinned against Him. In declaring, we admit to our wrong doing. A person cannot be helped until they admit their condition. Whatever your addiction is today, give it up. It is not worth an eternity in hell. Repentance is not a ritual that you should undergo so that "God will not get you," but it is a process that sorrowfully admits that you have sinned against the Almighty God. You have broken a bond and you want that bond restored. Once we repent, we will receive God's mercy. Jeremiah 31: 17-20 (New International Version) says:

17 *So there is hope for your future," declares the* LORD. *"Your children will return to their own land.*

18 *"I have surely heard Ephraim's moaning: 'You disciplined me like an unruly calf, and I have been disciplined. Restore me, and I will return, because you are the* LORD *my God.*

19 *After I strayed, I repented; after I came to understand, I beat my breast. I was ashamed and humiliated because I bore the disgrace of my youth.'*

20 *Is not Ephraim my dear son, the child in whom I delight? Though I often speak against him, I still remember him. Therefore my heart yearns for him; I have great compassion for him," declares the* LORD.

God wants us to repent. He sits back and longs for us to return back to Him. He instructed his disciples that a good shepherd would leave ninety-nine sheep to seek out the one lost. God loves us so much that he will do the same. No matter what you have done or what addiction you now have, God sees you as his child and nothing less. As the passage in Jeremiah shows us, God remembers our early relationship we had with Him and he yearns for that! When true repentance is sought, we will be able to experience the power of God's love that will break all chains that are keeping us bound. Acts 3:19 reminds us to: *"Repent ye therefore, and be converted, that {our} sins may be blotted out ..."*

> *No matter what you have done or what addiction you now have, God sees you as his child and nothing less.*

The second part is to forgive yourself. I know that it is hard, but in order to get healthy you must forgive yourself. God has already forgiven you, now it is your turn. God sees you only as His child; therefore, you have no right to see yourself as anything less. We forgive others, but we wear our guilt like a blanket. We walk around depressed, suppressed, and oppressed when God has already impressed unto us His Spirit. An African proverb says that if you can handle the enemy within, then the enemy outside can never win. If you will forgive yourself and move on, then battles you will encounter will not be strong enough to take you down. We have got to be happy with ourselves. My grandmother instructs the women at Pure Word to buy themselves flowers if their mate does not. She tells male and female to know who they are and to feel good about themselves. If we learn the simple principles of loving and forgiving ourselves, we are able to walk with our heads up. I can remember a few years ago I had gone against my grandmother and entered into a relationship that ended in my detriment. I was left heart broken and in debt. I had focused so much on making her happy that I neglected to make God happy. I wanted to spend more time with her than with God. Long after the relationship ended, I did not want to come to church. I did not feel worthy. I felt that I had let myself, my family, and God down. I had to come to the realization that I am human. Yes, my grandmother is the pastor, but I make mistakes too. I am a work in progress. Now, did that make what I did better? No, it showed me that it is so important to stay in the will of God. If we detour, we will lead to a road of destruction. Religious leaders today need to be more open and honest with people. People need to know that, yes, the preacher sins too. The common misconception is that once saved always saved. We tend to think that church officials, in any capacity, are exempt from sin. We are not. The important thing is to get back up and begin walking righteously. I read a sermon illustration from A. B. Earle's *Incidents Used* ...,which gives a great example of the importance of repentance. It represented our heavenly Father as telling a man, if he would bring up to the gate of heaven the most precious thing that could be found in this world, it would gain his admittance into heaven. "Then I am sure of heaven," he said. "I know what the most precious thing in the world is." He went to a mint where the best specimens of gold could be found, and obtaining the purest piece possible, flew up to the gates of pearl, sure that heaven would be opened to him, but found the gates closed and bolted against him. He was told that it was not the most precious thing; that their streets are paved with gold, as it was transparent glass. He came again. This time he obtained the most exquisitely beautiful specimen of jewelry, nothing richer or more beautiful on earth of its kind. He carried this up, but found the door still shut against him. He was told that no one used jewelry there. It was really of no value in heaven. He must go again. This time he was walking on the beach, under the shade of beautiful trees, thinking over what that most precious thing could be, when his attention was attracted to a beautiful little child lying on the grass under the shade of these trees, with its innocent face upturned towards heaven, in a sweet sleep. Just then a robber came to this little child, and stood over it for a moment, apparently in deep thoughtfulness, gazing on its innocent face, the child unconscious of any danger. The robber, reviewing his own life in his guilt and wickedness, and contrasting it with the innocence of that little child, drew a deep sigh of regret and sorrow over his life of sin, when a tear of penitence dropped from his eye.

The man in search of earth's most precious thing, caught this tear, and flew up to heaven's gate with it, when he found the gates thrown wide open to him, with a hearty welcome from the heavenly ones, saying:

> *"Yes, you have brought the most precious thing that can be found on earth, which is the Tear of Repentance." The point of the story is to respond to the call of God tugging at you to turn back. Don't be proud and feel that it is too late, accept God's Amazing Grace for no earthly treasure can connect you back with God.*

Lastly, receiving and experiencing forgiveness obligates us to forgive others as Christ has forgiven us. Many of us have not been able to move forward because we cannot forgive. In order to start loosing weight, you have to give up some things. Paul said, *"Forget those things which are behind and press toward the mark."* Peter asked Jesus how many times he should forgive those who had sinned against him. Jesus replied, *"I tell you, not seven times, but seventy times seven."* We must exercise forgiveness if we truly want to make a total commitment to Christ. Focusing on the past keeps you from moving toward the future. You have to learn to let it go. Paul had to do it. After all Paul went through, he asked God to remove a thorn. Many of us have asked God to remove our thorn(s). Yet God has replied, *"My grace is sufficient for thee: for my strength is made perfect in weakness."* (2 Cor. 12:9) Unforgiveness is one of Satan's spirits that we must overcome. We have the power to do it. This is a heavy weight that will suffocate our growth in Christ. With unforgiveness and Satan's other spirits in you, God cannot move in His characteristics.

One of the greatest illustrations of forgiveness in the Bible is the story of Joseph. Joseph had every right to be angry with God for allowing all obstacles to come to him, because of a dream. Yet, Joseph held on to God. Joseph saw that God always made a way for him. By the end of Joseph's struggles, God had allowed Joseph to be second in command to Pharaoh in Egypt. The Bible says that Joseph welcomed his brothers and father back into his life and moved them into the palace. Now the story has a greater meaning to it. Jacob's role is often overlooked. If you read Genesis 42 and 43 closely, you will see that Jacob had not moved on from losing Joseph. If he did not let go of Benjamin, he would not have received the blessing(s) of God. All the time, God was waiting to bless Jacob. Jacob's blessing(s) depended on one thing. He had to let go of the past. Today, if you do that you will be able to receive the things God has been waiting to give you. You must see your future with Christ better than your hurtful past. God said, *"I will turn your ashes to beauty."* (Isaiah 61:3) Therefore, I challenge you to let it go and turn it loose. If you let it go, God will take care of it.

You must see your future with Christ better than your hurtful past.

When I was in the seventh grade, I was officially adopted by my maternal grandparents. When I was in high school, I would see my friends' fathers and mothers pick them up and show them love. I was so jealous. I was jealous because God allowed them to have their parents I did not have mine. I thought it was unfair because I was "in the church." I constantly asked

God, "Why couldn't I have that?" I knew my grandparents loved me, but I longed for the love of my parents. I could not understand why my mother chose alcohol and drugs over loving me and why my preaching father could not even pick up a phone or even visit me. Those frustrations led to hatred. At some points, I even asked God to kill them. They both hurt me so badly. I was told that my father taped my mouth shut when I would cry and as a child I remembered seeing my mother struggle with her many addictions. Now that I have become an adult, I look back over my life and thank God for allowing me to go through that experience. Their abandoning behavior has made me a better person. Because I was in the house with my grandmother, I was able to be in the church. Through her teachings I was able to attend the best high school in Mobile County, UMS-Wright Preparatory School and later Spring Hill College. This situation presented countless other blessings. God is truly awesome. When I released my frustrations and gave them to God, He worked them out. He gave me beauty for all my ashes! Today, God's blessed me with a strong, healthy, relationship with my parents. My father and I talk about four times a week, and have been preaching together. It was hard letting go the hurt my parents had caused me, but since I laid that burden down, I feel better, so much better! If I never forgave them I would be just as guilty as them. God has commanded us to forgive. Without doing so, we cannot serve Him. My feelings with my parents were reconciled because I found reconciliation and love with God. In order to receive God's saving grace, you must experience his forgiving grace. We cannot receive Christ until we experience forgiveness. I had to come to the realization that if I wanted to grow in God, I had to forgive. In forgiving my parents, I was able to receive

God's amazing grace and his many blessings.

The writer of the famous hymn, "Amazing Grace" understood the concept of forgiveness and the power it has. John Newton was a slave ship owner and was known for abusing and even murdering slaves. He felt justified in his practices because he did not see the slaves as humans. One day while on the seas, a great storm arose and Newton and his men almost died. This near-death experience showed Newton that he was spiritually dead. However, one day he met the Lord and his life changed forever. He left the slave trade and later became a minister. Newton was so overwhelmed by God's Amazing Grace that he wrote:

> Amazing grace! How sweet the sound,
> That saved a wretch like me!
> I once was lost, but now am found,
> Was blind, but now I see.

> 'Twas grace that taught my heart to fear,
> And grace my fears relieved;
> How precious did that grace appear
> The hour I first believed.

> Through many dangers, toils and snares,
> I have already come;
> 'Tis grace hath brought me safe thus far,
> And grace will lead me home.

The Lord has promised good to me,
His Word my hope secures;
He will my Shield and Portion be,
As long as life endures.

When we've been there ten thousand years,
Bright shining as the sun,
We've no less days to sing God's praise
Than when we'd first begun.

Undergoing this "stretching" exercise will get your mind, body, and spirit man ready for the workout God has for us.

Before I move on, I want to point out a problem I do have with forgiveness. We abuse it. It is my sincere prayer that you appreciate God's forgiving grace. Today's world focuses so much on God's forgiving grace that they neglect experiencing his keeping power! That is why I wrote this book. The church has not taught people how to stay connected with Christ so that we will not fall. We are not to live saved just in the four walls of the church; we are to be a light that cannot be hidden. Folks in our homes, in our community, and on our jobs should know we are saved. Paul experienced the power of God as well as his forgiving grace. Paul and Newton did not abuse what they knew they could receive. We premeditate what we want to do because we say, "Oh, I can repent and God will forgive me." The devil is a lie! You need deliverance. Stop trying to figure how to get back up again. Work to keep from falling. Because when you fall, there are always consequences. I have a grandmother who has fallen down a flight of stairs twice in the past three years. In each fall, she was bruised and affected mentally from the fall.

Jude 1:24 reads, "*Now unto him that is able to keep you from falling and to present you faultless before the presence of his glory with exceedingly joy...*" God has power to save you and keep you from falling. You, as a child of God, have the same power of God. The world did not give it and the world cannot take it away. Therefore, if we learn to resist the devil, and his spirits, they will flee. It is time now to stop talking Jesus and start living Jesus. There is a blessing in serving God completely; ninety-nine and a half percent will simply not do. God does not bless mess. Through seeking God for true forgiveness, we will be able to move forward and walk in faith, because without faith, it is impossible to please God. And "faith comes by hearing, and hearing by the Word of God." Hence, through obeying God's Word, we are empowered to overcome the fiery darts of the enemy. Through his blood, we are able to cast down every strong hold. This power, not the altar experience, will keep you today and forever! Therefore, if you undergo a true confession of sin and let go of the past, you will be ready to workout.

Take forgiveness seriously, and after you are forgiven, focus on the power of God's keeping power. Because like stretching, if done right, experiencing forgiveness, for real, will make your work-out cramp free!

Chapter Two:
The First Exercise
Pull-Aways

L ike most exercises, this one has some side effects. Doing this exercise may leave you having to work-out alone. In order to do this exercise properly you have to pull away from those folk and things you should not be associated. I am reminded of a popular saying that says, "Birds of a feather flock together." In the legal world, innocent people are sometimes arrested because of whom they associate themselves with. They call it guilty by association. In order to prevent this from happening to you, you must do some pullaways.

Psalm 1:1 says, "*Blessed is the man that walketh not in the counsel of the ungodly, nor standeth in the way of sinner, not sitteth in the seat of the scornful*." In order to really understand what the Psalter is saying we must break down the verse in the original Hebrew. In the Hebrew, ungodly ('aviyl) refers to being morally wrong. These are people who are unjust. They are people who do what they want to do without concern for others. Sinners (chatta') refers to offenders. Sinners are people who do things they KNOW are wrong. Lastly, scornful (luwts) simply means to mock. The scornful are the ones always talking about God has not done anything for me, yet they are alive.

The best thing about pullaways is that it keeps you away from the spirits of these sinning, scorning, ungodly individuals. This exercise is mandatory for strength. The pullaways strengthens the spiritual muscles that help us to stay clear of these types of people. Whether you want to admit it or not, hanging around an infected person can, and will, make you sick. That is why you have to do pullaways. As a Christian, you have to stay clear of these types of people. If you do not stay clear, you will be infected. My grandmother is known for her declarations on this subject. If we are not pulling them in, they will pull us out. It is a tug of war. And the enemy is not going to give in. Proverbs 4:14-15 says, "Enter not into the path of the wicked, and go not in the way of evil men. Avoid it, pass not by it, turn from it, and pass away." Two things are a problem for some church folk: our ears and mouth. We say and hear everything and anything. We have such itching ears today that we flock to mess. We need to stop hearing so much garbage. The sad and pitiful thing is we want and like to hear things about our sisters and brothers in Christ. We seek to be a Holy Ghost inspector. We get on the phone and talk half of the night about folk, and come to church and act like we are holy and love everybody. We have it all wrong. We need to learn how to stop people from hindering our growth. Our souls are not garbage cans. Our bodies are the temple of God. When people bring you stuff you just need to say, "Let's pray about it." I guarantee you by doing that, you will not have many gossiping friends. We must remember that every day of our life is recorded by God. There is no editing of our actions. One day we are going to stand before a God, and we will have to answer to some things we have done. We have spoken our minds and listened for so long that we thing it is okay.

It is not. God is not pleased with this type of behavior from a Saint. I encourage you to make a list of some people and things that have been keeping you down. Examine that list and ask yourself, "Is it worth it?" Get enough strength to pull away from these things. It is better to cry now than later. If you know that after talking to certain people you are not up but down, then you know they are not a spiritual asset to you. You have got to tell people, "TMI (Too Much Information)." Instead of us talking about people and situations, we need to be praying! St. Francis said, "Preach the Gospel at all times; use words when necessary." St. Francis is basically saying we are to walk the walk and not talk the talk. Our actions should speak that of a Christian. We are to let people see our light. And they can only see the light when we are free. One of the things I have tried to look for in a friend is someone who can uplift me. In walking with Christ, we have got to make sure we are not associated with people who are not going anywhere. If we hang around people who are negative, we will start thinking negative. I believe the Prophet Elisha received a double portion of Elijah's anointing because he consistently stayed around Elijah. Elisha knew that Elijah had a true connection with God. No matter how Elijah told Elisha he could leave, Elisha stayed. We must do the same thing. Stay around godly people. Stay around people who are going somewhere in life and spiritually. You will be surprised that the more you hang around a person the more you begin to act like that person. Find people that have a moral code and are walking righteously with God. In order for God to be able to be in our midst with people, we must walk in agreement. The world says, "Opposites attract." However, the Lord is telling us, "Do not be unequally yoked." (2 Cor. 6:14) Jesus said in Matthew 18:20, "For where two or three are gathered together in my name, there am I in the midst of them." Those friends and things that are not godly will not be a dwelling place for the Lord. Therefore, you will not be able to grow. One of the hardest struggles I have had in my life is that of wanting to be accepted by people and "fit-in," but I had to come to the realization that I have a calling on my life, and that calling is priceless. This walk with God is going to require us to strip away any and everything that keeps us from living a sanctified (separated) life. I relate to the struggle the early church father, St. Augustine, experienced about finding himself. Like St. Augustine, I searched all over to find love. I never found the fulfillment to my void. This void was created from the beginning. Like St. Augustine, I had to come to the conclusion that only God is worthy of my love. As a church leader, I have seen people try to balance the world with their Christian walk and each time they ended back into the world. The world does not mean us any good. The enemy will fool us and have us thinking that our life was better in the world, but we have to keep our focus and say, "I have decided to follow Jesus; No turning back, no turning back!" There is safety in the boundaries of God.

Chapter Three:
The Second Exercise
Pull-Ups

No spiritual workout is complete without pull-ups. It is time to dust off the Bible and pull it up to our face. Do not look at it and skim it, but **read** it. The Bible is God's will and guidance for abundant living. It has our entire heritage and estate in it. In order to claim what is yours, you must read what God wrote. This exercise can be found in Psalm 1:2 which says, "*...His delight is in the law of the Lord; and in His law doth he meditate day and night.*"

Pull-ups build up your spiritual muscle, so that your spiritual body can burn the fat and calories brought on by the attacks from the enemy. In the spirit realm fat and calories represent:

- Trouble in your home
- The jealous folk on your job
- The low-down family members
- That child that is pushing you to the limit
- That sickness that seems to be overtaking you
- The mental battle you deal with every day of your life

- ANY ungodly spirit

The enemy is walking, seeking to devour us. He desires to see us disinherited. He wants us to fall and stay down. John 10:10 reminds us that *the thief, the enemy is come to steal, to kill, and to destroy.*

> *Because the enemy wants to take you out, he will do anything to keep your spiritual life filled with fat and calories.*

Because the enemy wants to take you out, he will do anything to keep your spiritual life filled with fat and calories. Pull-ups will put the devil on the run. My grandmother always tells the church that when the enemy is coming upon you, just put the word on him. The word will fix the problem. The enemy has been successful in attacking our minds. We must have a strong mind to defeat the enemy. That is why we are to have the mind of Christ.

- When the enemy tries to attack your mind, you start doing some pull-ups and you will find that the Word says, "*He will keep you in perfect peace, whose mind is stayed on thee: because he trusteth in thee.*" (Isaiah 26:53)

- When the enemy tries to attack your finances, you start doing some pull-ups and you will find that the Word says, "*And my God shall supply all of my needs according to His riches in glory.*" (Philippians 4:19)

- When the enemy tries to make you feel like you are a nobody, you start doing some pull-ups and you will find that the Word says, "*You shall be the head and not the tail you shall be above only and never beneath.*"

(Deuteronomy 28: 13)

- When the enemy tries to attack peace in your life, pull up the Word and remind yourself that Jesus can say, "*Peace, be still.*" (Mark 4:39) And after Jesus says that every thing in your life that is chaos must, and will, listen to his voice.

- When the enemy tries to attack you, and make you think that he has won, pull up Isaiah 54:17 which says, "*NO WEAPON that's formed against you shall prosper!*" It just will not work because God is with you.

The King James Version tells us to meditate on the word day and night. However, the Hebrew word for meditate means to speak to yourself. We have to learn how to speak blessings into our own lives. Many of us sit back and wait until some preacher, prophet, and bishop comes to town so we can "*get a word.*" We have the access to the Living Word; but we will not unleash Him in our lives. You serve the same God. Seek his face and get a word for yourself. When the enemy starts talking, bless God and remember your promises. You are too blessed to be stressed. The greater the test, the greater your testimony! It is through our trials and tribulations that we are able to help others. You must see your circumstances as a mechanism that is getting you closer to your goal. So, start telling the devil, "*I am Blessed by God's WORD!*" Remember: every knock-down is not a knock-out. And every stumble is not a fall. We often sing Timothy Wrights's famous song "*Trouble Don't Last Always,*" at Pure Word. It is an encouragement to stay in the fight. The devil may have won some battles, but he will not win the war.

The song says in one verse:

> May not come when you want Him,
> but He's on time (on time).
> In times of trouble, I find Him to be
> a friend of mine (of mine).
>
> When storm clouds rise in your life,
> He'll be there (be there)
> All your burdens,
> I know the Lord will bear (bear)

You can make it through the Word of God. I know the pain is deep and the tears keep flowing, but in the morning, it will be all right! Trouble cannot and will not last always.

Chapter Four:
The Third Exercise
Push-Ups

The third exercise is found in Psalm 121:1-2, which reads, *"I will lift up mine eyes unto the hills, from whence cometh my help. My help cometh from the Lord, which made heaven and earth."*

The key to this exercise is doing it on a consistent basis. You must do this even when you do not want to. The Word will strengthen us to walk around smiling when you should be crying; laughing when you are sad; and worshiping & praising God when your life is in a mess. In the midst of the trials, you must hold your head up. No matter what, you must keep your focus to know that you have one objective: TO DEFEAT THE ENEMY! This exercise helps us to strengthen our FAITH in God's Word. Therefore, we know that He is always present. The world says, "Seeing is believing," but a saint of God will say, "believing is seeing!" We have got to see our way already being made. We must see the chains being broken. We must see our blessing before it gets here. Life and death lies in the tongue. Always remember, "What a man thinketh, so is he." Our inner thoughts will influence our outer circumstances. If we walk around and say we are defeated, then we are defeated.

This exercise challenges work on push-ups constantly so that when life throws you a lemon you can make lemonade. If you start working on holding your head up, you will not have to worry about trying to hold your head up when trouble comes your way. Now if you do not have enough strength to hold up your head, just do one thing—leap for joy. The Bible declares that the joy of the Lord is our strength! Therefore, if we just leap, the joy will come, thus giving us strength. Philippians 4:4 says, *"Rejoice in the Lord always. I will say it again: Rejoice!"* We are to rejoice through it all. Yes, it is hard, but we must lift up our head and keep going. We cannot just sing; praise is what we must do. We have got to do it! The Apostle Paul understood rejoicing more than any other Christian I can think of. He truly went through many adversities. Just read 1 Corinthians chapter 12. God does not take part in pity parties. He has instructed us, through the Apostle Paul, to rejoice always! That means through the good and bad. One of my most encouraging verses in the Bible is Habakkuk 3:17-18, which explains, *"Although the fig tree shall not blossom, neither shall fruit be in the vines; the labor of the olive shall fail, and the fields shall yield no meat; the flock shall be cut off from the fold, and there shall no herd be in the stalls: Yet I will rejoice in the Lord, I will joy in the God of my salvation."* The prophet understood the importance of rejoicing. He did not give in to the enemy; he did something—HE REJOICED!!! It may have looked as if the situation was hopeless, but he knew if he changed his perspective on the situation, it would change. We too must do the same thing. We have got to change our attitude on things.

I am reminded of a sermon illustration about keeping your head up. It is about Road Runner and Wyle E. Coyote.

Wyle E. Coyote was always trying to get Road Runner. Sometimes, he was pretty close to catching up with him. However, in the midst of his running, Wyle E. Coyote would run until he ran out of road. He would be running so fast that after he ran out of road his legs would still be moving. In each episode Wyle E. Coyote made one big mistake. He looked down. It was at that moment that he began to fall. Road Runner, on the other hand, kept running until he got back on the road. If he had trained to keep his head up, Wyle E. Coyote probably could have kept going.

> *You must tell yourself that God has not brought me this far to leave me.*

I can remember talking to some runners. They told me that while they train, they learn how to keep their heads up. According to them, looking back slows them down. In order to out run the enemy, we must keep looking forward, because looking back will cause us to perish like Lot's wife.

Many of us face this same dilemma. On life's road, you will get to a place where you feel like you're losing ground. You feel that in any moment you will fall and will not be able to get back up. You feel that you are in the middle of life's ocean with no life jacket. However, you must call out to God just like Peter did on the sea and remember to "look to the hills whence cometh your help." You must tell yourself that God has not brought me this far to leave me. You may not see it or feel it, just know He is right there. Psalm 34:19 says, "Many are the afflictions of the righteous but the Lord delivers him out of them all." God has the power to deliver you from the hands of the enemy. There is a congregational song that says:

Leader: If you call Jesus
Congregation Replies: He will answer prayer!

What you've got to do is learn how to take your problems out of your hands and put them in the hands of the Master. In your hands your problem(s) stays the same, but in the hands of God it means being healed, set-free, and delivered.

- A basketball in my hands is worth a lost game. A basketball in Kobe's hands is worth a championship.

- Boxing gloves on my hands is worth me being beaten. Boxing gloves in the hands of Ali is worth being declared a legend.

- A golf club in my hands is worth a terrible score. A golf club in Tiger's hands is worth a Green Jacket and millions of dollars.

- Two fish and five small loaves in my hands is just a dinner. Two fish and five small loaves in God's hands will feed nearly 25,000 people.

- Nails in my hand would kill me, and you. Nails in the hands of Jesus saves the entire world from eternal damnation.

It depends on who is in control. We need to make Christ our head. We need to learn to put all our problems, not some, in the hands of the Lord. He will work them all out. Stop making God your "co-pilot." Make Him your pilot. If you do this, you will have a smooth and safe trip into Heaven! In John 15:4-11, Jesus instructs us to:

4   *Abide in me, and I in you. As the branch cannot bear fruit of itself, except it abide in the vine; no more can ye, except ye abide in me.*

5   *I am the vine, ye are the branches: He that abideth in me, and I in him, the same bringeth forth much fruit: for without me ye can do nothing.*

6   *If a man abide not in me, he is cast forth as a branch, and is withered; and men gather them, and cast them into the fire, and they are burned.*

7   *If ye abide in me, and my words abide in you, ye shall ask what ye will, and it shall be done unto you.*

8   *Herein is my Father glorified, that ye bear much fruit; so shall ye be my disciples.*

9   *As the Father hath loved me, so have I loved you: continue ye in my love.*

10 *If ye keep my commandments, ye shall abide in my love; even as I have kept my Father's commandments, and abide in his love.*

11 *These things have I spoken unto you, that my joy might remain in you, and that your joy might be full.*

In abiding in Christ, we will be able to walk in the abundance of Christ. That can only happen if we are spiritually fit.

Chapter Five:
The Fourth Exercise
Run!

One distinct characteristic of "black Christianity" is its music. It seems we have a song for every occasion or trial. At Pure Word, people will often hear Evangelist Cynthia M. Willis sing:

> Leader: RUN
> Congregation Replies: Don't Look Back

It is these types of congregational songs that speak to our lives. We are in a race for our current lives, and eternity. The Apostle Paul understood the concept of Christians running a race. To make sure the Corinthian Church understood that our spiritual life requires struggle, pain, commitment, and exertion, Paul uses a race as an illustration. Paul writes, *"Do you not know that in a race all the runners compete, but only one receives the prize? So run that you may obtain it. Every athlete exercises self-control in all things. They do it to receive a perishable wreath, but we an imperishable. Well, I do not run aimlessly, I do not box as one beating the air; but I pummel my body and subdue it, lest after preaching to others I myself should be disqualified."* (1 Cor 9:24-27—Living Translation) The ultimate goal of living as a Christian is eternal life. We have to continue to run, no matter what. We must be like Road Runner and keep running even if the road ends. We can never be like Wyle E. Coyote. In order to successfully win the prize for which we are aiming, we must keep looking forward while running.

I am reminded of the story of John Stephen Akhwari of Tanzania. In the 1968 Olympics, early during the twenty-eight mile run, Akhwari injured himself. Yet he continued to run, even though he knew he would not win. All the runners, except him, had crossed the finish line. So many people had left. However, before all were gone, sirens emerged. As peopled looked toward the sirens, they saw a bloody, bandaged, and hobbling fellow running toward the finish line. When Akhwari finished the race he collapsed and was rushed to the hospital for treatment. A few days later a reporter asked him why did he continue running knowing that he would not win and that he was injured? Akhwari replied, "My country did not send me 5,000 miles to start a race; they sent me 5,000 miles to finish a race." Akhwari understood who he was running for. He understood that he did not have to win the race or even get a medal. He only had to finish the race. In the letter to the Corinthian Church, the Apostle Paul likened the walk with Christ to a race. He says, *"Know ye not that they which run in a race run all, but one receiveth the prize? So run, that ye may obtain."* (1 Cor. 9:24) One of my biggest pet peeves is seeing people stop what they have started. So many of us have had dreams and allowed situations to stop us. We must remem-

> *We must remember that winners never quit and quitters never win!*

ber that winners never quit and quitters never win! So many of us, in the Church, have gifts and talents that we have allowed to die, because we have gotten discouraged by people. We have got to run so that we may see Heaven as our eternal home. We can run so that we can get praise and glory. Sadly, the church has become that way. The church now is a competition. We try to be like a certain preacher, singer, or dancer in the church, when God just wants you to be yourself. One of the things saints have got to learn is that the church is not a track arena; it is the House of God. We have gotten it so wrong. We think God is pleased, but he is not. Isaiah 64:6 reminds us, "But we are all as an unclean thing, and all our righteousnesses are as filthy rags; and we all do fade as a leaf; and our iniquities, like the wind, have taken us away." It is not about us.

I encourage you to keep going no matter what. It is when we are weak that God makes us strong. You can live a Christian fruitful life. The roads of life are filled with many bumps, but you must keep running. If we fail to run, we will not only be miserable on earth, we will be miserable for eternity. Running helps work the entire body. By running, our spiritual man is also getting into shape because we are leaving everything behind to follow Jesus. In order to serve God fully we must let go of stuff. We can run freely, and faster, with the weights off. Ask yourself today, "Who am I running for?" If you are running for the Lord, then you will do every-

> *You might not run as fast as others, but get yourself a steady pace and keep going.*

thing, you can to finish the race. You will run through the storm, the rain, the hurt, the "beat down," and anything else that comes along during the race. You cannot let anything stop you from running. You might not run as fast as others, but get yourself a steady pace and keep going. Ecclesiastes 9:11 encourages us by saying, *"The race is not to the swift, nor the battle to the strong..."* If you are running for the Lord, you will be able to finish the course because God will be right there with you. Isaiah 40:31 (NIV) says, *"But those who hope in the LORD will renew their strength. They will soar on wings like eagles; they will run and not grow weary; they will walk and not be faint."* We will be able to reap a blessing, if we keep going.

One of the things I was not taught early in the church is that church folk are an interesting group of people. I had to learn on my own that even the church has wolves. I can honestly admit that there is no greater hurt than being hurt by the people in the church. Earlier this year, I experienced some liver complications, and the pain I experienced does not compare to the hurt of the church. I have had to experience jealousy, lies, and phony people since I entered the ministry. At many times I wanted to give up. I cannot even count the numerous times my pillow was full of tears at night because of church folk. I have written at least eight resignation letters, but each time God told me to keep going. I have experienced suicidal thoughts, the "I just HATE church folk and do not want to have anything to do with them," and the "I ain't going back to that church" emotions. While I was up killing myself with worry, people were asleep. Even through all my trials, I have had to learn that I am not running for other people and not even myself. I am running for the Lord. When I decided to follow Christ, I also signed a contract to go through some stuff. This is a journey. We have got to be like the Energizer Bunny. We have to keep going, and going, and going. When I was a child, I had a clown bop bag. No matter how hard I hit that clown, the clown popped back up. That is how we must be today. No matter how hard the blows come, we have got to pop back up. I have seen so many people leave the church because of people. We have got to remember that every church has problems. There is no perfect church. We need to learn to stick situations out. My grandmother always tells me, "Cederick, you will NEVER be a great leader being a jelly fish. You must be strong." Her advice is confirmed in 2 Timothy 2:3: "*Endure hardship with us like a good soldier of Christ Jesus.*" I had to learn to be a thermostat and not a thermometer. A thermometer measures temperature. It is affected by its surroundings. On the other hand, a thermostat changes its surroundings. When the surroundings get out of bounds, it just kicks on. Dr. King, and other Civil Rights Leaders, would not have been successful if they would have turned around. They consistently sung, "Ain't gonna let no one turn me around!" We have got to infuse the same mentality they had in our walk with Christ. We cannot let anything turn us around. Running is so important. *We will reap if we faint not.* Jesus himself had to keep going when family and followers had forsaken Him. John 6:66 tells us that *many of his disciples went back, and walked no more with him.* Jesus understood His mission. He had to finish his course. Mark 3:21 reveals, "*When his family heard what was happening, they tried to take him home with them.*" "He's out of His mind," they said. Jesus knew that even though earthly family and friends had forsaken Him, He had a Heavenly Father that was pushing Him.

Second Timothy 4:7-8 encourages us to keep running no matter what. The writer says, "*I have fought a good fight. I have finished my course. I have kept the faith. Henceforth there is laid up for me a crown of righteousness, which the Lord, the righteous judge, shall give me at that day: and not to me only, but unto all them also that love his appearing.*" The Apostle Paul understood the concept of running for Jesus. He told the Corinthian Church:

> *21-23 Since you admire the egomaniacs of the pulpit so much (remember, this is your old friend, the fool, talking), let me try my hand at it. Do they brag of being Hebrews, Israelites, the pure race of Abraham? I'm their match. Are they servants of Christ? I can go them one better. (I can't believe I'm saying these things. It's crazy to talk this way! But I started, and I'm going to finish.*

> *23-27 I've worked much harder, been jailed more often, beaten up more times than I can count, and at death's door time after time. I've been flogged five times with the Jews' thirty-nine lashes, beaten by Roman rods three times, pummeled with rocks once. I've been shipwrecked three times, and immersed in the open sea for a night and a day. In hard traveling year in and year out, I've had to ford rivers, fend off robbers, struggle with friends, struggle with foes. I've been at risk in the city, at risk in the country, endangered by desert sun and sea storm, and betrayed by those I thought were my brothers. I've known drudgery and hard labor, many a long and lonely night without sleep, many a missed meal, blasted by the cold, naked to the weather.*

28-29 And that's not the half of it, when you throw in the daily pressures and anxieties of all the churches. When someone gets to the end of his rope, I feel the desperation in my bones. When someone is duped into sin, an angry fire burns in my gut.

30-33 If I have to "brag" about myself, I'll brag about the humiliations that make me like Jesus. The eternal and blessed God and Father of our Master Jesus knows I'm not lying. Remember the time I was in Damascus and the governor of King Aretas posted guards at the city gates to arrest me? I crawled through a window in the wall, was let down in a basket, and had to run for my life (2 Cor. 11: 21-33—The Message Translation).

While taking a theology class on the Early Church, I was able to learn a lot about the early church fathers. St. Polycarp caught my attention because of his endurance and faithfulness to God. He was martyred in 155 AD. He was to be nailed to a stake and burned. The government wanted him nailed so that he would not run away once they sat him on fire. St. Polycarp told the officials nailing him would not be necessary. He simply replied,(paraphrased) "The God that gives me strength to endure the fire will also give me strength not to move!" St. Polycarp, unlike us today, understood that being a Christian was more than a bumper sticker and cross around our neck. It was a practice of endurance. He was able to rise to the occasion when his faith was challenged. He was able to turn into a thermostat and change the situation. His faith was in God, alone. He knew that God's strength would see him through.

During the 1972 Olymipics, Dave Wottle shocked the world by winning the 800 meter race. Wottle had started out last, but managed to out run other runners in the last twenty meters. He won by three-tenths of a second. After the race, reporters asked him how did he win. Wottle replied, "The other runners went out so fast at the beginning that they slowed down at the end; I was able to maintain the same pace I started out with." Do not try to out run people and do not try to keep up with people. Find your pace and begin enjoying the run for the Lord. Trying to keep up with others will result in losing the race. You have come too far to loose now. Just keep going. Remember you are not running to win; you are running to finish.

Conclusion

As with a natural workout, one must do a "cool down" regime. Our cool down includes drinking water and reflecting on our present and future. Many of us have some "husbands" at home like the Samaritan woman. It is time to let go. Jesus said, *"If you drink of me, you won't thirst again."* Drink of Him Saints. We must realize that while undergoing this extreme makeover we are getting ourselves ready for the kingdom. We are one day closer to our appointment with eternal life. I want to do everything I can to be ready. How about you? I do not understand why so many of us have to get right when bad things happen. Let's look at ourselves in the mirror and say I am "stinky in the nostrils of God." I am sick and tired of being sick and tired. I must make a change. We all need an extreme makeover. One thing I have always admired about my pastor is that she will openly admit that even she, if she does not have her stuff together, will be lost. Saints, it is time to wake up. We are so far from the mark and do not even realize it. We need to be like Tonex and ask God to make us over again.

We need to humble down and ask God to put us on his wheel. The consequences of living an obese life are too high. Hell is too hot and eternity is too long. Let us just go through the struggle of making over our spiritual bodies now so that they won't be burned for eternity. I would rather whip myself into shape than to have God whipping me. What about you? Living for God is going to take sacrifice. Second Timothy 3:10 says, *"Yea, and all that will live godly in Christ Jesus shall suffer persecu-*

tion." This life will not always be full of good days, but, if we hold out, eternity in heaven will be worth it. God will repay right every wrong you endured for Him.

The direct message of this book is to get right or get left. The Apostle Paul instructs us that once we accept Christ, He will do two things in us. He will sanctify us and justify us. Sanctify meaning to set us apart from the World. And justify meaning to declare us righteous. We are to look like we are Christians. The workout in this book will put you on the road to get your spiritual life together. Christ is coming back and if we are not fully transformed, we will go to hell. After undergoing this work-out, I hope you are able to see that you were fatter than you thought. Undergoing this extreme makeover will make the word a reality in our lives. It is time to start walking the walk completely. There is no more time for straddling the fence. We need to search deep and ask God for help during this process of changing. If we sincerely mean it, God will come in and do a total change in you. He will tear up everything that is not like Him. Saints let us get it together. You can respond to God's Word in two ways. You can be transformed by a renewing of your mind, or you can dismiss it and continue living your way. Which person are you? Take up the cross and follow Christ completely. Start today by becoming spiritually fit! Eternity depends on it.

Note to the Reader

The publisher invites you to share your response to the message of this book by writing to C. D. McMillan in care of New Birth Publishing.

Should you desire Pastor C.D. McMillan to minister at an event, please, contact him via email at bookcdmministries@gmail.com.

www.ingramcontent.com/pod-product-compliance
Lightning Source LLC
Chambersburg PA
CBHW061158040426
42445CB00013B/1714